TOWER SERIES   NUMBER FIVE

Half Tame

To Debris—
   With love and
abiding faith in the
Vicious Fourth—
       Bettie
       December, 1965

Half Tame

Poems by

ROGER SHATTUCK

with woodcuts by   NAOKO MATSUBARA

THE   UNIVERSITY OF TEXAS

Austin

Some of the poems in this book have appeared in
Audience, Audit, Botteghe Oscure, The Hudson Review,
The Literary Review, New World Writing, Poetry,
Prairie Schooner, Quagga, The Texas Quarterly
Permission to reprint them here is gratefully acknowledged

Library of Congress Catalog Card Number : 64–64147

Published by
THE HUMANITIES RESEARCH CENTER
THE UNIVERSITY OF TEXAS
Distributed by
UNIVERSITY OF TEXAS PRESS, Austin, Texas 78712

Printed and bound in the United States of America

For NORA

CONTENTS

Today
this clearest coldest
day whose mirth is brittle
in the snow and rings space like a chime
there is no child or artisan
on earth could say
the sky is not
jet black

What stops me
hand and mouth to watch
this criss-cross tablecloth
the plate of smiling white?
A patch of shell anchors the bread in place.
The quarried egg with open veins
sings yellow in the dusk.

    Chardin Cézanne and Braque
    your craft has made a monkey
    of my eyes.

A glass of water stands beside
providing purity a theme to vary on.
These objects with two flesh-tight peaches
slashed by the knife's diagonal
compose a supper that my eyes fell on
before my appetite.

    The world I see tonight
    is quick
    and I am still.

For a Copy of
THE ANNOTATED ALICE

To Marc

Beware the looking glass, my son.
There, glassy-eyed and turned about
You'll see one wonder in the land
No one but you will think to doubt.

But HERE, fear not. No Snickersin
Can catch you if you have this book.
Read on, read off, look out, look in
To see, my son, just how YOU look.

For Keith

Chez Bertrand opposite the Institute
The customers' uncertain entry is dispelled
By kind attention from mine host.
He moves the chair, adjusts the implements and reads aloud
The simple bill of fare from *potage aux légumes*
To *poire, pêche, raisins* at the end.
The customers smile wanly and select
Their meal, including wine. Not until then
Do you, crouched in a corner with a *foie aux pommes*
Make out the customers are blind.

Chez Bertrand there are orange marigolds
Placed on clean tablecloths in gentle hope
Of sight for all who enter here.
Inside the Institute across the street
There is no thought of putting
Flowers in the rooms, and sometimes dust collects
And kicks unswept along the corridors.
In that gaunt building people don't, at dusk,
Turn on the lights and pull the shades.
Life perserveres in darkness.
But opposite, Chez Bertrand,
Everything is clean and colorful
And bright.

The reason I come back is that I know
The customers perceive my solitary soul
Across the room in every tiny sound
My knife strikes on the plate,
In how my lips talk to the food,
In how my feet talk to the floor.
For the duration of a meal I would believe
I am the man of whom they are aware—
A man unseen, but reached through senses
That are mirrorless and find affection
Without terror in the dark.

They murmur softly among themselves
With heads unturned to face the rest,
And push great chunks of omelette on their probing forks.
They dress and talk and tear their bread
Like any other Frenchmen, yet their eyes
Bespeak the presence of a space inscrutably profound
Or vacant in their lives.
Their hands reach cautiously for where they know
The bottle smoothly holds its cylinder of wine.
The gurgling weight swings down beside the orange marigolds
And fills the upheld shaping of the glass.
The glass rises to lips that wait in unmasked eagerness,
And look—
Look how the room and I are captured
In this drinking hand. Look at this slow
And quivering appreciation of the world.
Look at this sightless man and see,
See how the blind hear flowers in their wine.

I

Woman softly weeping to the sofa back.
    She never cries.
Man pacing, thinking with his lifted arms.
    His limbs are dumb.
Inside, the children sleep with drooping mouths.
    Their day is done.
A faucet drips, the macaroni cools.
    Love may be lost.
    Each night is long.

"Must I lose what I did not want till now?
    and still may not?"
"Only this wreck could rescue us," he said;
    he had grown strong.
"I cannot live by what I have not made."
    She fought to love.
"We made it all—even the reef we struck.
    Now we are wise."
"Why did you turn," she asked, "from me toward her?"
    Her eyes were closed.
"I never turned from you. I lost my way
    and have come back."
"Cold," she said. "I'm cold. When shall we know
    how lost we were?
    how much we lost?"

The children rise
to find the world still moored to clothes and toys.
    Moored in their bed
woman and man keep warmth between their thighs.
    He wakes alone
and walks in slippers through their house of shards,
    a chilly home,
to nudge the thermostats and bring the news
    in off the porch.
Heat comes up like water in the rooms
    and tides the day.
"Wake up," he whispers to the dreaming wife,
    "wake up, we're here."
They wade together through the grey-gold and
    reluctant dawn
to breakfast and the children's puffy eyes.
    "Come back, come back,"
she whispers to the wakeful husbandman.
    He goes to work.
    The day sets in.

When the night stands wide awake and panting in the street
the workers leave their strong-faced wives at home
The trattoria blocks the tiny square with tables
and the reek of wine   Under the lamp
two youths one sound and swarthy
the other withered back to dust below the waist
(his smile is wan to tell how Yankee bombers
dropped this childish stature on his life
He has the prowlike head and torso
of a centaur cheated at the pelvis
where the legs and love begin)
two youths caress the stir and sting
of their guitars and will draw blood
before the night is out
The tenor in an undershirt and jet black hair
waits with his eyes cast down for an elusive clue
The trattoria holds its breath
The candles barely quiver at their posts
Then suddenly he throws up his head
and drives the night back in the smoky streets

> *I like to sing this way*
> *This is my song*

The wrinkled women grin behind their litres of Frascati wine
and passing cyclists drop one foot to earth
to hear the stanza out
The tenor lifts his glass his eyes his voice
lifts all Trastevera in two sturdy arms
that fall with the cadence of his endless chant

> *You people are my friends*
> *I drink to you*

In his drinking we are drunk
as his song sings us into story
into his-story *stornelli*
songs of wine and music in the streets
tonight and here
this once for all

For a Copy of
THE OXFORD DICTIONARY OF NURSERY RHYMES

To Tari

A book of rhymes
For all the times
We want to know
How verses grow.

During those times,
Before we know,
These same rhymes
Can help *us* grow.

If you can grow.
If you can rhyme,
You've bested time—
So much I know.

LEGEND

For Alexandre Varille

I

Among the irrigation ditches and the goats,
As casual as fieldstone cast aside
To free a plough, the stiff Colossi sit
With half their pedestals sunk in fertile mud.

Each year the Nile must bury Egypt in her blood.

The Amenhotep giants guard the Theban dead,
And from their tall renown the Greeks contrived a God:
Memnon, Dawn's son, killed by Achilles' squabbling sword.
The Jewish Christ was not yet born or mocked the day
The restless classic gods revived their slaughtered son.
An earthquake danced the Theban mummies, all but unstepped
The two Colossi. The miracle was done. Thenceforth
When Dawn's first light, still fifty feet above the plain,
Touched Memnon's brow, a heavenly music issued from
The warming stone. Wayfarers told in Greece and Rome
How Memnon thawed to life beneath his mother's fond
Regard and voiced the triumph of the ancient deities.

All Egypt marches deathward on a temple wall.

The world made pilgrimage to hear the oracle
And scribble verses on the statue's knees.
Memnon sang joyously until a Roman
Emperor decreed the crevassed rock restored.
Memnon fell silent in the flat Egyptian fields.

I dreamed in Luxor that the priest was yelling
All the night atop his minaret. When I awoke
He chanted still his Arab anguish which alone
The day would dim. The crew that took me on the Nile
Seemed still to sleep beneath the languid sail.
We crossed, nudged by the voices of the windless stars.

The Theban sky is gold and lapis lazuli.

I had been told that half an hour's walk northwest
Would take me to the spot. The seven thousandth
Generation of Pharonic cock taunted
The glooming skyline while I raced the sunrise
Down the road. I thought I heard the sun's
First brimming rays awhisper overhead
And lowering slowly toward the land. I should have run
Except that all antiquity had fixed my pace.

The dawn in Africa growls long below the dark.

As I arrived the murky landscape tilted visibly
Toward earthquake; the faceless face of Memnon
Found the sun and floated, for a space, alone
In light and blind to fields below.
Across those flooded years of stark Egyptian silence
Came a music never blown or plucked
Or bowed on any instrument. Perhaps,
As with those sea shells in whose coils we listen
To the stirrings of our own dark sullen blood,
I heard only a spirit moving in myself . . .

What harm that I should name that spirit "Memnon"
Having come so far?

The god that rises daily with the dawn
Stirs not a limb for all the music in
His monolithic eyes. In death he scorns
The pilgrim at his feet, the tourist, voyager,
Voyeur, who worships at the wonders of the world
By taking photographs. But go behind
And see where out of sight a stake and cross-tree
Fix the torso, stiffen that thick neck.
In death he speaks another life. Memnon
Was crucified in stone.

A day may dismay
may's hopeful tale
of a springtime won
by planting a pole

The pole stood tall
the day I fell
through the season's thrall
into wantonness

Mayday mayday
I called to spring
and lurched in the sky
while the revelers sang

Mayday mayday
we murmured in mirth
for that day set free
our seasoned youth ●

MEANS OF EXISTENCE

(After Claude Roy)

What do you live on? A glint of day
the air of things the sun above
a breath of wind a fleck of sky
    cool water and on love

Who are you? A lost silhouette
a presence without anyone
what silence softly hums to none
    and all forget

What do you say? Nothing or nearly so
what words themselves can barely say
what silence takes to its own way
    when speaking low

from ASYMPTOTES
(After Renée Reise Hubert)

I. *The Doll*

Mornings she wore evening gowns
of a shrill and velvet elegance.
For her faults, all copied from my sins,
she was smartly spanked on her behind.
Evenings she paid calls in her carriage
returning courtesies to ladies and to rabbits.
Every children's disease that visited the street
stretched her on her bed under warm covers.
She had to swallow my infallible medicines
her cheeks all radiant under soiled lace.

II. *Prayer for My Doll*

Our Father who looks down from on high
protect my beautiful doll
for she is so very much afraid
of those terrible drops of rain

Our Father who looks down from on high
send down on us coins enough
to buy a big umbrella
My doll will be very careful
that it doesn't become too soaked

Our Father who looks down from on high
I make you a firm promise
that the day it truly showers
I shall lean far out my window
to gather up all the drops

COURANT POÉTIQUE
(After Renée Reise Hubert)

Faithful
        the blood circulates in the vein
on the grinding axle of routine

The reel of film unwinds without a whisper

The watch hand
forever behind
describes its vicious circle

While the trackless train
travels on and on
drawn into the same circuit

The earth is round and it turns

(After Olivier Larronde)

Full face in eyeless profile this writing rendered
    By your slope for limbs to ravish,
My voice is deaf to any other skirmish
    Whose singing leaves the air unsundered.

The massive ink inclines its porch, connives
    With light to splash time down the path . . .
In the immobility that mutes my mouth
    Skier or word, but one survives.

My long drawn ages, mastering their fall
    Take root beneath the scriptured snow
While clouds of me rise in a doldrum spell.

    Words on all sides hold their tongue,
Time stopped! except to trade the treacherous blow
    Your writings deal my swift aplomb.

For Tom

Here goes
as far as there
and then comes back to here
Mottoes
as thin as air
secure our verbal rear

The things we talk with change their skin
the minute we come near them
The ears and toes of complex words
grow faster than we hear them

To move from here to there
keep calm and stick
to prose
Poetry fans the air
poets are sick
heroes

No no you're wrong you lie
Verse can restore
our cheer
Joyless we live and die
anything more
goes here

here goes

Tornado Alley, May 1957

Like hell it's round
it's flat
and wet
    two months of rain leave Oklahoma
    in the bottom of the pan no gold
    but something else worth more and dirtier
Why don't you leeeehhuuuuvv me
twangs the radio
we'll do just that
but where's the surface on these greasy roads?

    The needle quivers just at 70
    I quiver just at 33
    too old to die young and not yet middle aged
    unknown but promising
    driving 1000 miles nonstop to Iowa
    to celebrate (100 years too late) *Les Fleurs du Mal*
    bee for Baudelaire in the Bible belt

Straight through from Dennison to Muskogee the pumps
the hammer-headed man-sized praying mantises
suck juice out of the dead frontier
it reeks of oil
and still the filling stations never change
26 and 28 "save three cents" like hell
that way
I figure maple syrup costs as much in Rutland
as in San Antone
it don't add up
free enterprise to feed the fat
distribute the wealth equitably among the rich
no use to try another burg for price or size or speed
they got us taped inside this continent
and turn out fifteen million twelvetone dreamlined traps a year
for folks to play cross-country crinkle-fender in
the only exit's through the roof the sky they call it
west of Illinois

blue water sky you know the limit
come on squirrel who cares let's spin this whitewall cage
let's chase the Indians and Greeks right out of I-oh-way
Osceola Oskaloosa Ottumwa Corydon Sigourney
redskins and eggheads the whole damn bunch
don't stop this side of Winterset or Centerville
it reeks of good old USA
    then wee-wee-wee-wee
    all the way home
Oh why do you take to the open road?
My wife's hair burns like brandy
What will you say when you grow old?
Baudelaire was a dandy

For Harvey

As is
is as
unknown
as is
the cause
of life
come up
from stone

OR

As
is as dead as
is
as long as is
is not a verb

Goddammit (yelled the printer)
As you were

St. Francis of Assisi
Moth-chaser Agassiz
found it was wise and easy
to take the world as is

The smart research assistant
hearing the dinner bell
tripped on the fourth dimension
and lost the world *tel quel*

As never was
As is

Off beat off base off Broadway
in the cold lobby before the show
unnerved by a fountain-urinal of squashed copper tubing
     dribbling forlornly in a vat
I watch a sheepish audience try to recognize itself
for the elite it would like to be
The middle class the country's greatest
is represented exclusively by minors
The rest of us majors play both ends against
     and despair of class

During the long ineptly timed *coitus interruptus*
they call "living theater"
a bunch of guys sit around somebody's pad
     and wait
for god, for the author, for a connection
     no difference
Jazz nudges the needle toward th greasy vein
salvation the cops and death loiter behind the bathroom door
     no difference
So I sit in the fourth row
and sweat my undershirt and taste my bowels
So there's the connection, a lousy joke
Till this four-letter play
     I never knew the meaning of the word
Till today I thought catharsis was an
               inner
                   moral
                         emotional purging
Not on your life, man
This stinking foul-mouth show
rams all the eloquence of ecstasy and pain
into one word
shit
over and over and over and over
     until you've had it

It makes a lovely New Years afternoon
I hope three hundred classless grownup minors
turn majors by this matinee
to shit their pants the old Greek way
and walk out safe and sticky into Sixth Avenue

I. *Six*

I only want to look
I am afraid so much
You must stay very near
I promise not to talk
I promise not to touch

Please may I whisper it
I want to see you bare
I want to know just how
you and I are not
at all the same down there

II. *Eighteen*

Tapered from neck to ankle
on a lathe of glass which spins a litheness
in your sun-sleeked and fast flesh
strut baby undismayed beside
my pride and wear your pastel face
for me alone
           I want to see you
dressed to kill all challengers
the shopping-center royalty
the squinting motorcycle crowd
and every eye that swings our way
With your cool lips insinuating hair
and thighs unchafed inside tight jeans
kill them O baby kill them dead

Then afterwards alone alive
be lithe for me and in our only
home a car parked just across
the line from all your blandishments and mine
alive alone undressed kill me

III. *Forty-two*

I am the darkness where your beauty shines.
Your light slants shadows out of things, like sunrise
on a sleeper's lips, and I behold
a round and rendered world, your art, my obstacle
which girdles us. All our benighted days
we've raised the roof of domesticity;

all our bedazzled nights will never lay
the longing lurching laughing ghost of lust.

Five years adrift, we thought possessions were
the enemy. Planted in rented rooms, with friends
for furniture, we let our branches be our roots
and sap, like Spanish moss, the atmosphere.
Till offspring begot us here, twelve states away
from where we wed, in this our bank-blessed home
and pasturage. Our rearing children toss
and tease us up toward parenthood; with shouts
we tumble back, unstrung, to our old journeying.

At seventeen our marriage pits its youth
against our middling age and holds its own.

IV. *Sixty*

The fire never dies.
It burns along the bone
and hoards its heat beneath
the ashes of a man.
My milk and mica eyes
peer at a naked world
of well clothed animals
trained in the art of wanting
something else. Like them
I spent a wanton youth
in presbyopia
watching far-off green hills
turn grey when brought to heel.
And then one day I stumbled
into paradise.

I used to fear the matron
shrew or spinster sown
in each girl's fresh-tilled field
of flesh. Today I watch
the shining girl you wear
inside your face, the girl
age keeps for me alone.
And we are, no, not anywhere
the same, but we are one.

At ten to eight
citizen Harry Clemson, contractor,
began the Sunday morning service
of his drowsy wife, Elaine,
a rousing rite twice interrupted
by dear Marianne, aged four
    and hungry.

At eight fifteen
pewholder Clemson, murmuring the responses
stood for the collection hymn
and dropped his offering in the plate.
Then skirting his neighbor's outstretched knees,
for Clemson was known to be polite,
he slipped out unedified but still uplifted
    before the sermon.

At ten to nine
buxom Elaine called from the kitchen,
found master-builder Clemson
at work on the terrace unfolding
a sturdy semi-collapsed castle
of unstressed scriptural newsprint
peeled from the five-inch Sunday yule log
felled weekly at the door. Marianne
lay green and scarlet to the elbows
in the comic strips. Coffee
and pancakes could not lure King Harry
from his counting house, so breakfast
came to the King, who gave his Queen
This Week. They sat in state
till afternoon, when chicken, ice cream,
the lawn to mow, and neighbors dropping in
made a shambles of the sabbath scene.
    Alas.

    At nine p.m.
after standing each other all the day long
till faces lengthened and evening came
and darling Marianne was hushed
and Sunday was over and the dishes done,
then, in their great misfortune, brave Harry
and virtuous Elaine were granted the misery
of a television set. While a comic
gabbled at the automated audience
and the wide world shriveled to a twelve-inch dream,
daddy gave mummy a drink to nurse,
mummy gave daddy a neck to kiss.
Their poor hearts turned with one accord
to bed and love and rest and sleep
and Monday waiting there to take them in.
    Amen.

You said it
I couldn't have
                    ever
When I asked you if it hadn't been
        a good day
        a real fine
        (really)
        Saturday
you said
            with chocolate all over your chin
            and your big
                            blond
                                    nine-year-old
            grin
yes daddy (oh daddy!)
it was
        oh it was
Swimming and dessert
I loved it today
So
    and just so
                    can I
love it today
when you catch Saturday
like that for me
            your wings in the water
            the world in your mouth
            and you in this house
        my beautiful
        oh my dutiful
    bountiful
daughter

I've asked, and no one knows a name for them.
I'm not so old as to remember things
others forget. Still, my mind wears a contour
modelled by the way the land lay then.
In Wilton, Conn. (New England by
a wooded mile I know the inches of)
the backroads rose like stairways on the hills
and stepped as gently down again around
the sumac and stonewalls. A slope was built
of steeps and flats in turn, of work and rest.
The long pull strains the heart of man and beast.
To move a meadowful of hay the farmers
broke the back of hills and built for all
a terraced world to take their breathers in.

We summer people stayed our season on the slopes
and called them rollercoaster roads.
Our weekend fathers in their younger days
took the bumps like hurdles through the afternoon
and lifted us screaming off the rumble seat
one weightless instant into summer's orbit.

That was a generation and a war away.
Graders have made a clean sweep since.
The farting sports cars roam the countryside for prey.
Weekends I haunt my yankee father's ghost.

That scudding summer afternoon my brother Fran and I played
  catch in the front yard.
Mother said to watch for rainbows to the East.
The empty rockers watched us from the porch.
Two fields away the Stanard boys were lofting ricks of rye
  aboard the wagon, and the plump load raised their old man
  hoarse and stamping toward the spitting clouds.
We eyed the hay, the sky, and too infrequently the ball.
I had to chase it once under the maples into tall grass across
  the road.
That black hump ran the ridgeline like a spine between stone
  walls, a straight stretch up to Ruscoe's farm where the Green
  boys' flivver missed the curve one night and burned.
I stopped there on the pitted crown . . . cool air, the smell of
  dust, and down the center a misty margin where the greying
  tar turned black and slick as ice.
The rye grass whispered when I raised my palms to see.
"Look Fran, it's raining over here."
It was.
Our laughter sprang from disbelief.
We turned the axis of our game and tossed the ball through
  what we'd found—
no rainbow, just a line mapped on our landscape, I in rain and
  you in shine.
We couldn't stop laughing.
Till then the start of rain had been a moment in our lives, a
  murmur on the roof, a change of mood that signaled slickers,
  or sometimes popcorn, attic romps, and cards.
And now we'd seen it was a place bounding the countryside,
  another kingdom coming on.
The loaded wagon lurched between us like a precipice; you
  yelled and tossed me a high one.
The tiny planet rose and turned there in the sun above old
  Stanard's hat.
He sat half dozing on the rumbling float and fished for his
  horses underneath the bank.
As if agreed we left our game and ran to stand upon the road
  astride that front, or back . . . that edge of time.
We laughed no more and waited for the place to move, for
  mother's call, for rain.
They finally did.

My brother lives an ocean plus a continent away.
The letters we play catch with show our failing arms, our
veering dreams.
Thirty years have set all boundaries between us since we stood
before that summer house
expecting rainbows, finding rain.
It was a moment in an ancient afternoon
when we laughed as brothers and fell still.

I have two good dreams:
     One
     that all the brass in Christendom and Muscovy
     the politists and strategicians of the world
     wake up one morning with cracked tongues and thumping
         hearts
     and see what they've been doing.
     A housewife, a student, and a minister of God
     will knock that day at the palace gate
     and tell them firmly to
     STOP studying war.
     And they'll stop.
     And that will be that.

     The other good dream
     leaves the waters muddied.
     It is
     that nobody has the Bomb
     and Bluff is all.

And I have seven bad dreams
that are all variations on one:
     Someone up there
     a good husband and father
     earnest and kind in all his dealings
     Church member and music lover
     above party,
     one of the experts in weapons
     has troubled the others in the councils of state
     by speaking in symbols of a new high barbarism.
     He uses a blackboard with skill.
     At night he plays a game of odds and ends against himself
     and to his huge delight
     the game always wins.
     While waiting for the others to come round
     for the system to have a chance to prove itself
     for the lesson to be taught
     for the odds to become ends
     he retracts the colored lead in the four barrels
         of his automatic pencil
     and releases it, scupulously
     only as needed.

When asked these days
I say I sleep badly
but it may be just the opposite.
Nerval said he was learning to direct his dreams
so they called him mad and found him hanged
	from a lamppost.
All considered, devils drugs and doctors,
it looks as if we might master our dreams
	before our hands
and survive on the side-effects of madness.
Let us be crazy
like students and housewives
and holy poets.

For what seemed years
she was like that.
When you pointed out a rainbow to her
stabbing your finger toward the dark above the trees
she would look with wide attentive eyes
at your finger
and then, smiling, into your eyes.
You felt like a fool.
Such a lovely girl
at two.

Later I saw her, a lissom nine
light the stove with a match
blow out the match
and stamp her foot
because the burner had gone out too.
She went through it once more, the whole routine
singed her hair to boot
and still didn't see
that she'd blown it out herself in the same puff.
She was the fool this time
and frowned at my laugh.

How long can I laugh at Patricia? At nineteen
She walks in a world fractured by accidents.
At every corner she hears whistles
and all too often squealing brakes, glass mixed with screams.
She supposes it's the same everywhere
and has learned to live with it
accompanied by sirens and slaughter
wincing often, herself unharmed
still beautiful.

Seen from the train
the lights at the crossings are always flashing
and cars waiting.
The world is safe yet askew at the center of the whirlwind.

Wherever she enters
everything is suddenly different
because she has come, radiant.
But she is aware only of a stillness in the place
and thinks she has missed the boat
that the star has just walked out.
How could she know it will never be so
for she is herself that vessel of grace
that star of disaster.

Ah Patricia
you will never find peace
till you are old—
and even then I wonder.

They say you fled the Tzar and cheered the revolution
    till it turned on you
But that's not the escape we marvel at
What innocence or craft let you win through to us
    untouched by the homosexual palace guard that for two
        decades claimed all talent
    uncaptured by the salon princesses commissioning culture
        with the haute cuisine
    and unspoiled by enough books read to fog a scholar's brain

Between St. Petersburg and la Suisse Romande
you must have found the tonic for your life and time
so that today you walk unsinged
        in the furnace of serial composition
the way you perch unharmed in Hollywood
        where all souls perish

Maestro
    in your blue beret
your figure shows no distance
        from the peasant poking in his vineyard
        to the reigning Prince of Festivals
Bursting with eighty years of life you reach us
starting creation all over again from scratch
        annually
    and so sure of it you can flood it

Santa Fe, August 1962

THE FUTURE OF ROMANCE
A Texas Pastoral

In air-locked housecars
flank to flank they sit deprived of nothing
munching gum in shiftless splendor
stuck to the seat and to each other.
Public lovers on a rear-vision roadbed
god knows what they do in private
except crawl inside each other's skin
or separate just far and long enough
to telephone for another date.

After seven months of steady going
with a transistor set to keep them warm
at last they reach the drive-in marriage lot
and park.

They never wrote a love letter
nor saw the reason to.

For sunburn
she had an old remedy
                        and preventative
olive oil rubbed on the skin before going out
and at night
vinegar sprinkled over hot-cool flesh
It worked as well as any bottled stuff
and made a world of difference
                        to me

    That summer
two weeks evenly distributed
between the beach the bar and bed
I learned what the old poat was driving at—
        salad days
                        he said

NEGATIVE PREGNANT

For Luis Martin-Santos (1924–1964)

The sisters strapped me flat legs high akimbo
My half-sedated jesting that they might
deliver me of child in that position
barely held my head above humiliation
till the needle turned me off

Reformed rebored I lay five days afasting
in a tender ache and won release
to castor oil and belladonna for
the newborn king whose rank lubricity
was daily dressed by holy hands

I have produce no offspring in the Clinique
Sainte-Thérèse but got me big life
again and ready for bowls of food and wine
rowdy for trips to Corsica and Spain
ripe with everything but child

Our federal fathers tippling law and language
knew a negative pregnant from a bouncing babe
This primadonna patient took disembowelment
for self-delivery and ripped the cord   Force feed him
deadly nightshade for his lordly lapse

I have a place
just above the knee
when I wear shorts I pick at it
no mole or scar or pimple
a quarter inch of greying flesh
and over it a parchment skin
cancer? maybe leprosy?
    I pick at it
enough to strip off a shred of me
and turn the grey
    all red
it's always there when I wear shorts
the garden spot of my left leg
summer resort for an idle mind
in pants I never notice
    a few wild cells

I have a trick
of thinking my way is best
to fix the shades or slice a loaf of bread
or find the shortcut home
the wife gets sore
"You think you're always right"
she'd rather do it her way
and take longer
she didn't marry me for tricks
    not those tricks

I do a wicked lindy when I'm drunk
    sober
I limp like a crippled lobster
so I fell yes fell for a dancer
to spite my feet and spoil my pride
and the rest came tumbling
    after

Otherwise
     I'm normal
     half tame
to see me
you might even think I was easy
to live with

I wrote this poem
not at all like this
maybe one day
I'll be able to tell the truth
first off

750 copies of
Half Tame
have been printed and bound by
The Printing Division of
The University of Texas
Design & typography by
Kim Taylor
1964